AZTEC LIFE

BY
JOHN D. CLARE

Who were the Aztecs?

At its height in AD 1519, the Aztec empire covered 200,000 sq km (125,000 sq miles) of land, and contained at least three million people, who spoke more than 20 different languages. Tenochtitlan, the capital, was one of the biggest and most beautiful cities in the world. The Aztecs never called themselves Aztecs (although we will refer to them as such in this book). They were the Mexica – vicious, half-civilized nomads who invaded the area we now call Mexico in about 1100. It was not until 1325 that they came to settle in Tenochtitlan (*'Place of the Prickly Pear'*). Aztec culture grew, flowered and died in less than two centuries. The Aztecs never lost their violent nature, presiding over an empire that was an oppressive, bloodthirsty tyranny. Their culture was, in the words of one Spaniard, *'Butchery unequalled in history'*.

A WELCOME SIGN

The Mexica were nomads for many years, but in about 1300, they settled in a town named Culhuacan. There they sacrificed a local nobleman's daughter, and cut off all her skin. Horrified, the local inhabitants drove them out, so they fled to a nearby swamp. The next day, they saw the sign they had been waiting for – an eagle, on a cactus, eating a snake. They settled in the swamp, and built the town of Tenochtitlan.

CHANGING IDENTITY

Izcoatl, the first Aztec ruler, disliked the idea that his people were barbaric nomads, and destroyed all the writings which said so. Instead, the Aztecs claimed that they came originally from the same place as the Toltecs, a place they called Aztlan. There, so their legends claimed, Huitzilopochtli, the god of war (shown right), had told them to set off to find a new home. They would know they had found this place, the god told them, when they saw an eagle resting on a cactus eating a snake.

FIERCE BEAUTY

Historians are puzzled by the Aztecs' culture. In some ways it was colourful and beautiful, but it was also bloody and barbaric. This turquoise mask is beautifully made, but had a sinister purpose. It was used in an Aztec religious ceremony, and the person who wore it was probably sacrificed and eaten!

TOLTEC TEMPLES

When the Aztecs migrated to Mexico, they found the remains of past civilizations. They discovered Toltec temple ruins, which contained huge statues, like the one shown here at Tula, the Toltec capital. Such architecture amazed the Aztecs, who decided to copy the ways of these ancient peoples. In 1427, they asked Izcoatl, a local prince who claimed to be descended from the Toltecs, to be their ruler.

AZTEC EXPANSION

There was no farmland, wood or stone in Tenochtitlan, but there was salt (important in a hot country) and water, and there were birds, fish and frogs to eat. Slowly the Aztecs grew more powerful, and conquered neighbouring peoples. The Aztecs liked to pretend that they had a great empire, but they were never all-powerful. They ruled with the help of two other cities, Texcoco and Tlacopan, and there were some towns that they never conquered. This picture shows warriors from Tlaxcala successfully repelling an Aztec attack.

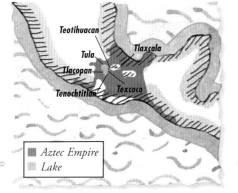

THE AZTEC EMPIRE

This map shows the Aztec empire at its height. The Aztecs ruled directly over the Valley of Mexico around Tenochtitlan, but they also dominated surrounding tribes. The Aztecs allowed tribal leaders to rule over their own people, but they demanded large tributes (payments) from them in exchange.

Teotihuacan
Tula
Tlaxcala
Tlacopan
Tenochtitlan
Texcoco

■ Aztec Empire
■ Lake

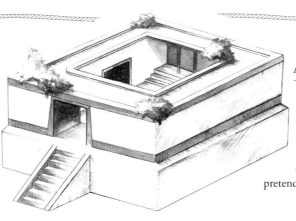

A NOBLEMAN'S HOUSE

Nobles formed a very small percentage of Aztec society. They were a highly elite group with special privileges that were fiercely protected by law. Only nobles could live in two-storey houses, for example. Any commoner who dared to pretend to be a noble was sentenced to death.

GOLDEN MYTHOLOGY

A nobleman was expected to be modest, holy and fond of the old traditions. However, the strict laws that existed against nobles who were adulterers and drunkards show that some may have chosen to behave more recklessly. The mythology expressed in this gold pendant perhaps offers a clue as to why they did this. It shows Mictlantecuhtle, the lord of the dead, who was believed to rule the hells beneath the earth. Souls who reached the land of Mictlantecuhtle were destroyed for ever, so some nobles decided, in the words of an Aztec poem: *'We are only here on Earth for a while, come let us enjoy ourselves.'*

MONTEZUMA'S PALACE

This Aztec drawing shows Montezuma's palace in Tenochtitlan. Inside, Montezuma sits alone in the throne room, while below are the meeting rooms for his generals (left) and his advisers (right). Montezuma's officials (tecuhtli) were expected to work, but in return they were given a fine house and lands, were paid large salaries and were exempt from paying taxes. The most important was a man called the Snake Woman (named after an important fertility goddess). He was the chief minister who looked after the everyday affairs of government. In the Aztec empire, only the nobles (the pipiltin) could become government officials.

Life for the Rich

The Aztecs conquered many cities, which were then forced to pay tribute. This meant that huge amounts of valuable goods flowed into Tenochtitlan, including blankets, military outfits, beads, feathers, dyes, gold, cotton, peppers and spices, sacks of maize and cacao beans, salt and many other things. Some of these were used in public ceremonies, some were given to the nobles and some were given to the local merchants, who traded them for other goods. Tenochtitlan soon grew into a very wealthy city.

MONTEZUMA II

At the head of Aztec society was the tlatoani. He was king, chief priest and commander of the army. In 1502, Montezuma II became the eighth tlatoani of Tenochtitlan. Nobles who went to see him had to take off their fine clothes and put on cheap blankets. They had to enter barefoot, with eyes cast down, and bow three times, saying: *'My Lord, my great Lord!'* Turning their backs on him was forbidden; instead, they had to walk out backwards. Montezuma II ruled from 1503, until he was murdered in 1520 following the arrival of the Spanish a year earlier.

A NOBLEMAN

The position of nobleman was hereditary. The only other way that a noble could be created was if the tlatoani raised a great warrior to the position of Jaguar or Eagle knight (see page 23), but Montezuma II put a stop even to this.

TRIBUTE ROLL

Tribute rolls showed the amount and type of taxes that had to be paid by provinces to the Aztec capital. The Aztecs used symbols for numbers – a dot meant 1, a flag meant 20 and a feather indicated 400. The various symbols illustrated the type of goods that were to be sent to Tenochtitlan.

Life for the Poor

HOUSEHOLD GODS

In every home, the mother made a shrine with a mound of dough to imitate the temple pyramids (see page 30/31). There she burned incense and offered food to copy the rituals at the temple. These figurines may have represented gods, but they are often found with their heads deliberately broken off, so they may have represented victims who were 'sacrificed' at the household shrine.

Aztec society had a strict class system. The tlatoani was at the top, with the pipiltin (nobles) below him, followed by the macehualtin (the citizens). The macehualtin were free, although the word means 'subjects'. They were organized into calpulli (groups) of about 100 households. Each calpulli had a council of elders who kept the register of citizens, shared out the land and collected taxes. The Aztecs believed that a boy became a man when he reached the age of 20. He was then expected to marry, after which he and his wife would be registered as citizens.

Nothing ever changed; people stayed in the class into which they were born and Aztec children were cut on the chest to show which calpulli they came from. The Aztecs were violent and warlike towards other tribes, but in their own society they did as they were told.

PEASANT HOUSING

Aztec peasant houses were built in groups of up to five, and faced each other round a courtyard. They had mud-brick walls and roofs thatched with leaves from maguey plants. Between five and eight people from one or two families lived together in a house. The houses were so small that most activities, including cooking and eating, spinning, grinding corn and socializing must have taken place outside.

SLAVES

At the bottom of society came the slaves (the tlacotin). Slaves were given as tributes by conquered cities. Some were criminals whose punishment was to be made slaves. Sometimes peasants, ruined by drink, gambling or disaster, would sell themselves into slavery in exchange for a loan to the rest of the family. Slaves could only be sold on if they were lazy – but the third time this happened, they were sold to the temple for sacrifice! This picture shows Chalchiuhtlicue, goddess of water, being attended to by slaves.

PEASANT POSSESSIONS

Poor families had no furniture and only simple clothes. The few essentials they did own included a metate stone for grinding maize, several pots and a sleeping mat. However, in recent times, archaeologists have unearthed large piles of rubbish outside peasants' houses, including imported pottery, obsidian knives, grinding stones and even bronze pins. Aztec peasants may have been poor, but because there was plenty of work and money flowing into the empire, few were totally destitute.

ESSENTIAL POTS

Even the poorest Aztec families needed pots – a water jar, a bowl for soaking maize, a flat grid for cooking, storage jars, plates, cups and at least one three-legged cajete with a criss-cross pattern on the bottom, for grating chilli peppers.

A HARD LIFE

The macehualtin produced the food, built the roads, temples and palaces and did extra work for the nobles. They paid taxes to the government officials to maintain the temples and schools, and they gave to charity to help the widows and orphans. Half of Montezuma's income came from the ordinary macehualtin. The macehualtin were not allowed by law to wear fine clothes, but this peasant, sitting in his loincloth, looks happy enough.

Food & Drink

The Aztecs were expert farmers. Most houses had a large garden (a calmil), and the tlatoani even had a botanical garden, where his gardeners grew plants, such as tropical flowers and cacao trees. There were no horses, oxen, wheeled carts or ploughs, so everything had to be done by hand. In the hills, the Aztecs built stone walls and created flat terraces for growing crops. In the hot valleys, they built aqueducts to bring water from the mountains. The tlatoani controlled all the water, which was one reason he was so powerful. The Aztecs' diet included things that seem surprisingly modern, such as popcorn, hot chocolate and roasted peanuts. Even so, food was not plentiful, and Spanish writers have written that the Aztecs ate *'as little as anyone in the world'*. Ritual cannibalism was so common that some historians believe human flesh formed an important part of the Aztecs' diet.

FAVOURITE FOODS

The Aztecs ate a surprisingly varied range of food. Particular favourites included kidney beans, sweet potatoes, avocados, maize, squash, chilli peppers, red, yellow and green peppers, tomatoes, mushrooms, duck, fish, rabbit and snails.

PULQUE GOBLET

The law forbade everyone but old women to get drunk, but at weddings people were allowed to get merry on pulque, an alcoholic drink made by fermenting maguey sap (see opposite). Only the rich could afford chocolatl, a drink made by boiling caca beans and honey. Some rich Aztecs also smoked tobacco, holding their nose and sucking in the smoke. Montezuma (see page 5) liked to finish each day with a cup of cocoa and a smoke. Some Aztecs took drugs called peyotl (made from cactus buds) and teonanacatl (a bitter black mushroom) which caused hallucinations.

CULTIVATING MAIZE

Maize was the main food in the Aztecs' diet and was planted each May. The farmer made holes with a stick called a coa and dropped in each seed individually. In July, all but the best ears were picked from each plant. The full-grown cobs were harvested in September. The maize was ground down to flour and made into round cakes called tortillas, which were eaten with every meal.

CHINAMPAS

In the swamps near Tenochtitlan, the Aztecs dredged mud from the bottom of the lake and piled it up to make fertile allotments called chinampas. Along the edges, they grew willow trees to make strong banks. The lake also provided a good source of fish, water-fowl and even blue-green algae, which was made into small cakes.

MAGUEY PLANTS

The maguey plant was important for the Aztecs. The tough stem made good firewood or strong fence posts. Its leaves were used as fuel for fires and stoves and also for thatching roofs. The leaf fibres were used to make the rough cloth worn by the peasants, and also for rope, paper, sandals, nets, bags and blankets. Maguey sap was used to make a sweet syrup or for pulque, and the spines made perfect nails and needles. Even the grubs which ate the leaves were a tasty treat!

FOOD FROM THE GODS

The Aztecs believed that all food was given by the gods, and held three festivals to help the maize grow. In May, the seed was blessed in the temple of Chicomecoatl, the goddess of corn, seen here with one of her attendants. In July, the young cobs were offered to Xilonen, a maize goddess. In September, a harvest festival was held, when a priestess dressed as Chicomecoatl threw dried seed at the crowds. People tried to catch some to add to the seeds they were keeping for the following year.

Pastimes

VOLADOR CEREMONY

In this religious ceremony, men dressed as birds, because it was believed the gods themselves could take this form. The men swung round the pole and the rope gradually unwound and lowered them to the ground. The length of the rope was calculated so that they reached the ground in exactly 52 circles. The ceremony represented the unification of the two Aztec calendars, which happened only every 52 years (see page 27).

For the Aztecs, religion was not just important, it was central to their whole existence. Even when they stopped working, everything they did had a religious significance. Aztecs did not have leisure activities in the way that we do today (purely for enjoyment). Aztec adults enjoyed the festivals and games described here, but their purpose was not simply to have a good time. Everything they did had a meaning, and was designed to fit in with the will of the gods.

AZTEC ORCHESTRA

Most Aztec music involved community chanting and stamping to the beat. The main instrument was the huehuetl vertical drum, and its name (pronounced way-waytl) gives a clue as to the sound it made. Another important instrument was the teponaztli, a horizontal round drum which was hit with rubber-tipped sticks to make two different-sounding tones.

PLAYTIME

Aztec children were only allowed to play with their toys until they were three or four years old. From this age, boys had to begin fetching water, and girls started to help their mothers around the house.

POETRY OF LIFE

Nahuatl was the Aztecs' language. The Nahuatl word for poetry meant 'flower-and-song'. Most Aztec poetry was written to the god Tezcatlipoca, the giver and taker of life, and in many poems, the ideas of flowers and song and life and death are linked:

'You come out from the flower and song; You scatter the flowers, You destroy them.'

This painting shows Xochipilli, god of music, poetry, dancing and flowers. The Nahuatl word xochitl does actually mean 'flower'.

BALL GAMES

Tlachtli was a tennis-like game in which players used their hips, knees and elbows to strike a large rubber-ball. If a player hit the ball through one of the raised hoops on the side of the court, he won outright. Tlachtli was a popular spectator sport, but it had religious meaning and losers were sometimes sacrificed. The game was also used to foretell the future. When the ruler of Texcoco prophesized that strangers would soon rule Mexico, Montezuma played tlachtli with him to prove he was wrong. Montezuma lost the game 3-2, and left the court a worried man. Two years later, in 1519, the Spanish arrived.

PATOLLI

Patolli was a gambling board-game. Players threw dice to move, and the aim was to get three counters in a row. Even this simple game was played to please the gods. The 52 sections on the board represented the years of the most important Aztec calendar. This picture shows a game being watched by Macuilxochitl, the god of plants and fun.

HAIRSTYLES

Aztec women loved to dress their hair, and dyed it black with mud or deep violet blue using indigo. The usual hairstyle was two plaits, brought round the front of the head and fastened together at the forehead. However, this statue of an Aztec goddess shows a style in which the hair is gathered into bunches at the side of the head, and worn with a braided headband. Hairstyles were important for Aztec men, too. Young men aged between 10 and 15 shaved their hair, leaving only a pigtail at the back of the head. They were only permitted to cut off the pigtail when they captured a prisoner in battle.

MAKE-UP MIRROR

This mirror is made of obsidian, a black volcanic glass. Aztec fathers told their daughters not to be obsessed with their looks, and not to use make-up – but they were ignored! Rather than enhancing natural beauty, the Aztecs used make-up to more dramatic effect. The face and body were thickly painted red, yellow, blue or green. For Aztec women, the fashionable complexion was yellow, and they rubbed their faces with a yellow ointment called axin, made from crushing the bodies of insects. They also stained their teeth bright red, and anointed their feet with fragrant oils.

NOBLE DRESS

This nobleman wears a coloured cotton cloak, decorated loincloth, sandals and an expensive necklace. Rich men sometimes wore many cloaks, one on top of the other, to show off their wealth.

FINE FEATHERS

Feathers were such an important part of a noble's costume that they formed part of most tribute rolls (see page 5), and feather-working was a major industry. This picture shows Montezuma's headdress. The feathers were pushed into bamboo tubes, and sewn together using a thread made of cactus fibres.

Fashion

The Aztecs did not have fashion in the modern sense; that is purely to look attractive or up-to-date. In the Aztec empire, dress, like everything else, had a meaning – it was a statement to the world of someone's wealth and status. What an Aztec could wear was set down by law. The macehualtin were forbidden to wear coloured cloaks, cotton cloth or gold jewellery. If a person even wore a robe longer than the law allowed, others would look at his legs – if these showed battle scars, the matter was dropped, but if they did not, he was put to death. Most poor people wore only a loincloth; if they could afford a cloak, it had to be a rough, white blanket made from the maguey plant. At the other end of the social scale, only the tlatoani could wear turquoise-coloured clothes or jewellery.

VERSATILE COTTON

Cotton could not be grown in Tenochtitlan, so it had to be imported from low-lying areas of Central America. As well as being an important fabric for clothes-making, cotton was used for bedding, bags, wall hangings, battle dress and burial shrouds.

JEWELLERY

Aztec nobles wore as much jewellery as possible – lip pendants, nose plugs and earrings of gold and precious stones. This earring is comprised of a gold skull bone and tiny bells.

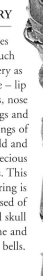

TEOTIHUACAN STONEWORK

Five hundred years before the arrival of the Aztecs, a great city had existed in The Valley of Mexico. It was called Teotihuacan, and was situated approximately 80 km (50 miles) northeast of Tenochtitlan. When the Aztecs migrated to Mexico, they saw the city's ruins and were so impressed that they decided it was the birthplace of the gods. They adopted many things from Teotihuacan, including its pyramids, its grid pattern of streets, its gods Tlaloc and Quetzalcoatl and the practice of human sacrifice. Rich Aztec nobles decorated their palaces with stone carvings (such as the one in this picture), copied from the masonry of Teotihuacan.

THE TEMPLE AREA

This drawing shows the temple area in Tenochtitlan.

This was the main temple, with its twin shrines to Tlaloc, the god of water (on the left) and Huitzilopochtli, the god of war (on the right).

A GRUESOME GODDESS

This statue represents the awesome goddess Coatlicue, the mother of Huitzilopochtli (god of war), so its symbolism is gruesome. She wears a necklace made of a skull, severed hands and human hearts, her skirt is a mass of writhing snakes and her feet are huge animal claws. However, her breasts are bare, and – where her head has been cut off – blood pours forth in the form of serpents. These details show the power of Nature to punish but also to nourish.

The temple of Quetzalcoatl (the god of priests) is in the centre, with rings like the coils of a snake.

The priests' quarters. This building also housed the calmecac school (see page 20)

Art & Architecture

STONEWORKERS

Aztec quarrymen could cut 40-ton slabs of rock by driving wooden wedges down cracks in the rock. Teams of labourers then dragged them to the building site, where they polished them and used metal chisels to carve the details.

Aztec art and architecture was designed to remind people of the power of the gods and the strength of the Aztec empire. In about 1500, the Aztec capital Tenochtitlan had to be rebuilt after being destroyed by a flood. It became a city designed to impress strangers. Reached by two causeways which crossed the lake from the mainland, Tenochtitlan was built on a strict grid pattern, with the main street running east to west, to mirror the passage of the Sun across the sky. Aztecs believed it was the centre of the Earth, and this poem reflects their sense of achievement: *'Proud of itself is the city of Tenochtitlan. This is your glory, O Giver of Life. Who could conquer Tenochtitlan? Who could shake the foundations of the Earth?'*

The small platform on the right was for gladiatorial sacrifices. A captured warrior would be tied there and given a wooden club. A fully-armed Aztec warrior would then fight him to the death.

The skull rack was situated next to the tlachtli court. One Spaniard calculated that the rack contained 136,000 skulls of sacrificial victims.

The tlachtli court (see page 11) was situated next to the temple of Quetzalcoatl.

GRASSHOPPER

This pretty grasshopper was a symbol of Chapultepec ('Grasshopper Hill'), situated just north of Tenochtitlan. The Aztecs stopped here during their time of wandering (see page 3). Chapultepec was also important to the Aztecs because of its springs of fresh water, which were taken by aqueduct to Tenochtitlan.

Health & Medicine

*T*enochtitlan had no working animals and its houses were built a good distance apart, so it was a healthier place to live in than European cities of this period. The Aztecs also had a good standard of personal hygiene, unusual for the time. They washed often, using the cleansing properties of the soap-tree fruit. Montezuma had a swimming bath in his palace, while many ordinary families had small bath-

AZTEC DOCTORS

Aztec doctors could carry out a range of treatments, such as massaging aches, stopping bleeding, stitching up wounds and setting broken bones. However, they believed that it was an evil spirit that had caused the patient to stumble, so as they set the bone they chanted a spell.

houses. Aztecs cleaned their teeth using salt and powdered charcoal, for they knew that not doing so resulted in tooth decay. They also checked each other's hair for lice. If someone became ill, the Aztecs had trained doctors who examined the symptoms and then prescribed a cure. Although Aztec medicine was a primitive medicine, the knowledge and skills of these doctors enabled them to cure some Spaniards whose illnesses had defeated European doctors.

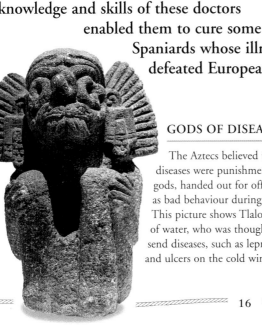

GODS OF DISEASE

The Aztecs believed that most diseases were punishments from the gods, handed out for offences such as bad behaviour during festivals. This picture shows Tlaloc, the god of water, who was thought to send diseases, such as leprosy and ulcers on the cold winds.

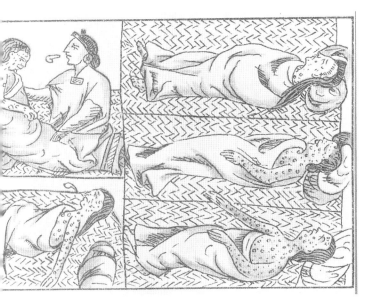

SMALLPOX

When the Spaniards came to Mexico, they brought with them new diseases, such as smallpox, to which the Aztecs had no immunity. This caused the deaths of millions of native Aztecs in the years after the Spanish conquest (see page 31).

MEDICINAL PLANTS

A good Aztec doctor knew how to use more than 1,500 herbal medicines. To treat a sore throat, for example, the doctor would prescribe a throat massage with liquid rubber, followed by a cough syrup made of honey and the syrup of the maguey plant.

FATES IN THE CRADLE

This picture shows the beautiful goddess Chalchiuhtlicue, the sister of Tlaloc and the goddess of clean water and childbirth. The Aztecs believed the fate of a child depended on the day it was born, and that some children were destined to be sickly and others to be healthy (see pages 20/21).

MAGICAL CURES

To diagnose a disease, doctors often administered a dose of peyotl (see page 8). This would cause the patient to become delirious and cry out, thus 'revealing' the cause of the disease. If the cause was thought to be the anger of the gods, the cure would usually be prayers and a strange symbolic medicine, such as crushed quartz or the spray of a skunk. If the cause was an enemy's magic, doctors known as 'worm-drawers' would rub the affected spot, 'pull out' a stone or a worm from the patient and declare the patient healed.

Love & Marriage

Girls as young as 10 years old got married in Aztec society. On the day of the wedding, the girl's parents gave a feast. The bride bathed, washed her hair and put on her wedding garments. When it was dark, the marriage procession set off for the groom's house.

Women with burning torches led the way, and the matchmaker carried the bride on her back. Once there, the matchmaker 'tied the knot' – literally tying the man's cloak to the girl's blouse.

Marriage was important in Aztec society, and an unmarried man could not become a citizen. Men were allowed to have as many wives as they could afford to support. Marriages were arranged by the parents, who decided on future matches when their children were still young. An older women acted as a go-between, seeking permission for the proposed match from the girl's parents. After marriage, roles for men and women were clearly defined. The man built the house and earned the wages. His father advised him, *'Do not be lazy, for then you will not be able to support your wife and children'*. A woman's job was to run the home. Aztec mothers told their daughters: *'Obey your husband cheerfully. Do not scorn him or be irritable, for you will offend the goddess Xochiquetzal'*.

XOCHIQUETZAL

Xochiquetzal was the goddess of beauty, love and marigold flowers (which represented the cycles of life and death) – but she sent boils to anybody who offended her. Aztec stories told of the tragedy that ensued when Xochiquetzal lost her virginity and was consequently thrown out of heaven. Distraught, she spent her time gazing up at heaven, and became blind with crying (the Aztecs believed this explained why people cannot look at the Sun). Similarly, if a girl was not a virgin when she married, the wedding would be cancelled and the girl's family disgraced.

MARRIED COUPLES

Women had separate roles to men, but they were not
treated as inferior. Men spent much of the year working
away from home, and during this time their wives were
in charge of the household. A woman could divorce a
husband who abandoned her or was violent, and the
law gave her half his land and possessions.
Although marriages were arranged,
most couples grew to love each other
and were happy. This picture shows
a man and wife sharing the important
job of storing the maize.

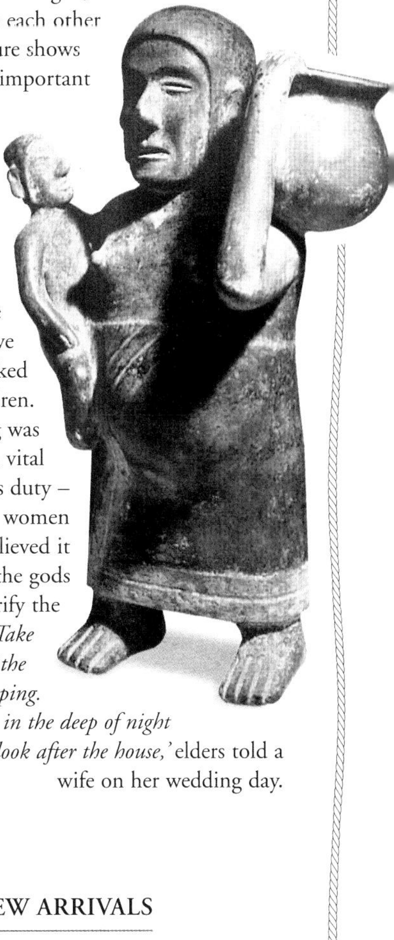

AZTEC WOMEN

Aztec women cleaned
the house, made
the meals, wove
cloth and looked
after the children.
Sweeping was
seen as a vital
religious duty –
Aztec women
believed it
helped the gods
to purify the
world. '*Take
care of the
sweeping.
Get up in the deep of night
to look after the house,*' elders told a
wife on her wedding day.

NEW ARRIVALS

Aztec couples wanted children, and
a barren marriage usually ended in divorce.
During the birth, the midwife shouted out battle
cries, symbolizing the mother 'fighting' to bring the
child to birth. Astrologers were consulted to foretell
the child's future based on its birthday. As the midwife
cut the umbilical cord, she gave the new baby a speech.
If it was a boy, she told him that he must be a great warrior,
who would feed the Sun with his enemies' blood. A girl was told
to spend her life doing the housework.

Children

The law required every calpulli, or group of households, to build schools for teenagers. Girls were taught how to sing and dance at the religious festivals, while boys helped with building work and trained to be soldiers. Noblemen's sons went to advanced schools known as *calmecacs*, where they learned about war and religion, but also studied history, medicine, mathematics, the calendar, astrology and law. There were strict rules for behaviour, and punishments were harsh. Boys who drank or ran after girls were shot with arrows or thrown into the fire alive. Aztec girls were expected to show great modesty, and had to look down at the floor at all times. Aztec education taught children to obey. They were indoctrinated to think like everyone else, not to think for themselves. No one was allowed to be different.

PUNISHMENTS

Punishments for Aztec children were very harsh. This father is holding his son over a fire and forcing him to breathe in the fumes of burning chilli peppers. The speech comma tells us that the child is also being given a long lecture as he is being punished.

SYMBOLS

The *Codex Mendoza* was a collection of drawings of native customs and tributes compiled for the viceroy of Spain after the Conquest. The illustrations in the Codex about bringing up children (shown on page 21) use the following key to show age and food. The red counters represent the age of the child, while the yellow chips illustrate the number of tortillas they were allowed to eat per day. This was an indication of the maturity of a child.

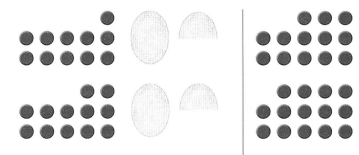

A BOY'S EDUCATION

Education for Aztec boys centred on learning
skills that they would need in later life.
They also needed to be able to operate boats
and canoes in order to work on the chinampas.

*This disobedient son, aged 12, has
been stripped naked, tied up, and thrown
into a muddy puddle in the street.*

The father is lecturing him.

*Here, a farmer is teaching his
13-year-old son how to carry loads
and how to handle a canoe.*

*These were essential skills for a farmer when working
on the chinampas.*

*This picture shows a farmer teaching
his 14-year-old son how to fish.*

*At this age, the boy would have been eating two tortillas a day,
so it was important that he earned his keep.*

A GIRL'S EDUCATION

Most Aztec education for girls took place in the
home. From a relatively early age, a girl would be
taught vital skills that she would use on a daily
basis in her role as a homemaker in later life.

*At age 12, a daughter would be
taught to grind maize and make
tortillas - the first job she would
undertake every morning when
she became a mother herself.*

*At age 13, this girl is being taught
how to sweep the floor. Sweeping
was a vital religious duty.*

*Aztec women believed that, when they swept up,
they were helping the gods to purify the world.*

*Weaving was a woman's job in
the Aztec empire. Here, the mother
is teaching the 14-year-old girl
how to use a backstrap loom.*

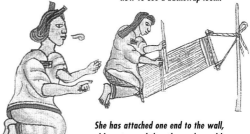

*She has attached one end to the wall,
and has strapped the other end round her
back. By moving backwards and forwards,
she can tighten or loosen the threads.*

War & Weaponry

The Aztecs were a fierce, military people who glorified war, as this Aztec poem reveals: *'There is nothing like death in war, So precious to the Giver of Life. I see it: my heart longs for it!'* The expansion of the Aztec empire depended on war. Its history taught that Huitzilopochtli, the god of war, had told the Aztecs to leave Aztlan and conquer the land. The empire's economy and wealth depended upon tribute payments from conquered cities. Above all, the Aztecs believed that the gods needed a constant supply of blood sacrifices to keep the world from falling apart, and wars were a good way to provide the victims.

A DEADLY CEREMONY

The Aztecs went to war not simply to conquer other peoples and gain tribute, but also to capture victims for sacrifice. In the ceremony shown in this Aztec painting, the captives were forced to dance all night, and were burned at the stake the next morning.

PROTECTION

A warrior's shield was probably made of wood covered with leather, and decorated with feathers stuck on with bat-dung glue. It would probably have afforded only limited protection during battle.

DRESSED TO KILL

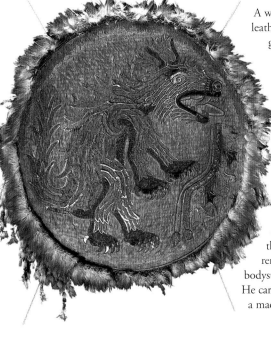

Each calpulli sent a regiment of men to fight in the army. There was no uniform; each soldier dressed as he wanted. This warrior wears sandals, a coloured skirt, a feather headdress and underneath, a thick quilted cotton bodysuit. The whole costume was so impractical that he would probably have removed everything except the bodysuit and sandals before fighting. He carries a thick two-sided sword-club called a maquahuitl that was so heavy that it could cut off a horse's head with one blow.

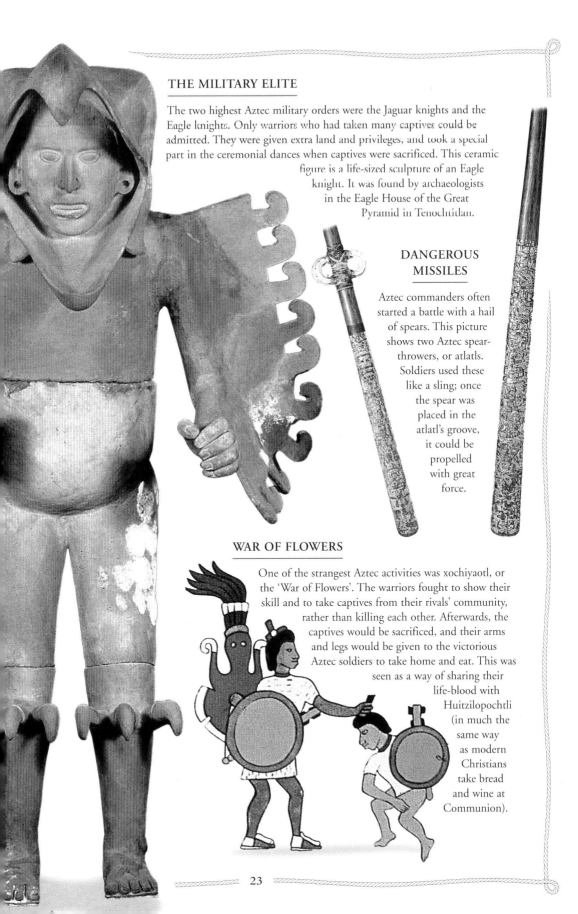

THE MILITARY ELITE

The two highest Aztec military orders were the Jaguar knights and the Eagle knights. Only warriors who had taken many captives could be admitted. They were given extra land and privileges, and took a special part in the ceremonial dances when captives were sacrificed. This ceramic figure is a life-sized sculpture of an Eagle knight. It was found by archaeologists in the Eagle House of the Great Pyramid in Tenochtitlan.

DANGEROUS MISSILES

Aztec commanders often started a battle with a hail of spears. This picture shows two Aztec spear-throwers, or atlatls. Soldiers used these like a sling; once the spear was placed in the atlatl's groove, it could be propelled with great force.

WAR OF FLOWERS

One of the strangest Aztec activities was xochiyaotl, or the 'War of Flowers'. The warriors fought to show their skill and to take captives from their rivals' community, rather than killing each other. Afterwards, the captives would be sacrificed, and their arms and legs would be given to the victorious Aztec soldiers to take home and eat. This was seen as a way of sharing their life-blood with Huitzilopochtli (in much the same way as modern Christians take bread and wine at Communion).

Trade & Travel

Aztecs loved going to the market (tianquiz) – 60,000 people went to the great market of Tlatelolco (situated just outside Tenochtitlan) every day. One Spanish priest wrote that, *given the choice between going to market and going to heaven, the normal Aztec housewife chose heaven, but asked if she could go to the market first!* The Aztecs were extensive traders, and their merchants (pochteca) were a separate class within Aztec society, each possessing their own calpulli, like a series of guilds. They also had their own god, Yacatecuhtli, whose symbol was, appropriately, a traveller's walking stick. But the Aztec pochteca were not upwardly mobile like today's businessmen. They had to keep to their place within Aztec society in the same way as the macehualtin.

MONEY BEANS

The Aztecs used cacao beans as money (though some fraudsters made forgeries out of wax or dough), so only the richest people could afford to drink chocolatl (see page 8) – the modern equivalent would be smoking cigarettes made out of £10 notes!

AZTEC SHOPPING

This picture shows an Aztec market (tianquiz) in Tlaxcala. Goods, such as meat, vegetables, herbs and so on were arranged in separate aisles, a little like a modern supermarket. Customers could buy not only the produce of the chinampas (see page 9), but also other foodstuffs which included dogs, iguana and wild turkeys from the valleys and oysters, crabs and turtles from the coast. They could also purchase many other things, from cotton and slaves to shells and gold. The Aztecs sold by quantity rather than by weight. Traders and customers usually bartered for goods, so the tianquiz must have been full of noise and argument. Government inspectors made sure goods were set out properly, and cheats were punished.

NOBLE TRANSPORT

The Aztecs had no horses, so a common form of transport was the litter. Here, a person impersonating the god Xochipilli is being carried on a litter in a religious procession, but nobles and rich traders also used this form of transport.

PORTER

Trading expeditions were dangerous undertakings. The pochteca were the only people allowed to cross borders into other states as the government found them useful as spies. Traders took weapons, and sometimes ended up fighting the people with whom they had gone to trade. Everything had to be carried, and the Aztecs used porters who – like the one here – wore head-straps rather than backpacks to bear the load. Before they set off, the pochteca would meet together and make offerings to the gods in return for their continued health and safety.

CANOES

It seems likely that the Aztecs did not use wheeled vehicles, although some historians disagree. Canoes were therefore essential for carrying heavy goods into Tenochtitlan, and the canals formed the city's main 'streets'. Destroying Aztec traders' canoes was regarded as a declaration of war. After an expedition, the pochteca would smuggle their goods secretly into the city at night. Aztec commoners were not supposed to flaunt their wealth, and merchants wore plain clothes and kept secret how much money they had made.

LIZARD

SERPENT

EAGLE

RABBIT

WATER

DOG

MONKEY

GRASS

REED

OCELOT

Science & Technology

*T*he Aztecs had only the most basic technology, and they had no alphabet, using picture symbols called glyphs instead which were also used to represent the 20 days of the sacred calender (shown on the left and right-hand borders). Yet the beauty of their creations was bewitching. One of the first Spaniards to reach Tenochtitlan enthused: *'It is like the enchantments they tell of in the old legends!'* One historian attributes the success of the Aztecs to the fact that they learned to use simple tools with great skill.

AZTEC POTTERY

Aztec potters did not use a wheel; instead, they built up layers of rolled clay, and then crafted the pot with their fingers. They had no knowledge of glazes; most Aztec pottery made in Montezuma's time had black designs painted directly onto the clay surface. Rich Aztecs, however, preferred to use pottery made by the non-Aztec people of Cholula, a city 160 km (100 miles) east of Tenochtitlan. Cholulan pottery was multi-coloured, and included drawings of feathers, knives and skulls.

ANIMAL MAGIC

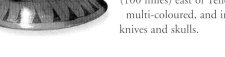

Aztec stone workers made jewellery and religious figurines out of alabaster, jade, turquoise, amber and obsidian. The stone-workers of Tenochtitlan persuaded Montezuma to go to war against certain cities, to increase supplies of the emery sand they used for polishing the stones. The Aztecs loved nature, and animals were a favourite subject for carvings, like this beautiful vessel in the form of a hare.

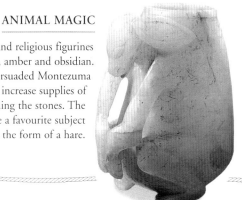

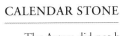

CALENDAR STONE

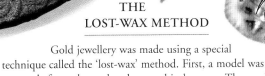

The Aztecs did not have a scientific explanation of how the world was created. They believed that there had been four failed 'worlds' before the present age, and that the gods Tezcatlipoca, Quetzalcoatl, Tlaloc and Chalchiuhtlicue had each in turn become the Sun, but had then been destroyed. The Aztecs believed that they were living in the 'fifth sun'. This huge, 24-tonne calendar stone (left) measuring almost 4 metres (12 ft) across, shows the fifth sun, Tonatiuh, at the centre. The four squares in the centre show the four 'failed' suns. The inner ring contains glyphs representing the 20 days of the sacred calendar, and twisting beyond this are the two fire serpents, whose heads meet at the bottom of the circle.

THE LOST-WAX METHOD

Gold jewellery was made using a special technique called the 'lost-wax' method. First, a model was made from charcoal and covered in beeswax. The model was then coated in a paste of charcoal and clay. As the hot metal was poured into the mould, the wax melted, and the metal flowed into the space in the desired shape.

THE NEW FIRE CEREMONY

The Aztecs used the solar year of 365 ¼ days, but for religious rituals, they used a sacred calendar of 260 days. Every 52 years the two calendars coincided, and the Aztecs believed this meant there was a danger that the world would end. Five days before the end of the cycle, everyone began to put out their fires, clean their homes, throw away their old clothes and smash all their pots. On the fifth night, people and priests marched to the Hill of the Star, and sacrificed a victim by lighting a fire on his chest and burning his heart. The Aztecs believed that these actions saved the world from destruction.

VULTURE

FIRST KNIFE

FLOWER

HOUSE

RAIN

MOTION

CROCODILE

WIND

DEATH

DEER

Religion

THE GREAT TEMPLE

At the centre of Tenochtitlan was the huge temple called the Templo Mayor. It was extended on seven occasions; by the time Montezuma came to power, it measured more than 90 m (270 ft) by 70 m (210 ft), and stood 27 m (81 ft) high.

Four days after it was born, a child's naming ceremony took place. As was customary in Aztec society, guests gave long speeches to the infant. These speeches were often depressing: *'You shall see and know and feel pain, trouble and suffering. This earth is a place of torment and toil.'* The Aztecs believed that both women who died in childbirth and great warriors became gods who helped the Sun to go across the heavens. People who died of disease or through accident went to the land of Tlaloc. Everyone else had to undergo torments on the way to Mictlan (the place of the dead), where their souls were destroyed.

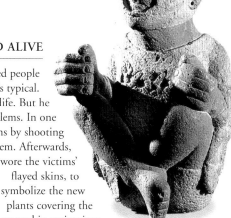

SKINNED ALIVE

Aztec gods, like Nature, hurt and helped people arbitrarily. Xipe Totec, the flayed god, is typical. He was the god of fertility, flowers and life. But he also brought skin diseases and eye problems. In one sacrifice to this god, priests killed the victims by shooting arrows at them. Afterwards, they wore the victims' flayed skins, to symbolize the new plants covering the ground in springtime.

THE COYOLXAUHQUI STONE

According to Aztec stories, when Coatlicue gave birth to the god Huitzilopochtli, her eldest daughter, Coyolxauhqui, climbed up the holy mountain to try to kill her mother. Huitzilopochtli leapt from his mother's womb, cut his sister into pieces and threw her down the mountain. This stone, found by archaeologists at the foot of the stairs of the main temple, shows her dismembered body. The story explains why after most sacrifices, the victims' bodies were thrown down the temple steps.

PRIESTS OF DEATH

Aztec priests wore black cloaks and grew their nails and hair long. Their hair was matted with blood, and they stank of rotting meat. Their duties were to make sure that all the ceremonies and sacrifices were carried out correctly. Some also taught the young noblemen in a school called the calmecac (see page 20). Others were scribes or astronomers. Aztec priests never married, and were expected to live holy lives.

GIFTS TO NATURE

The Aztecs belived that sacifices were necessary to make the Sun rise again; sacrifice was the 'pay-back' which fed the gods. Huge numbers of victims were killed – 80,400 were said to have been sacrificed at one ceremony alone. Ornate knives like the one above were crafted for such grisly purposes.

SACRIFICIAL RITES

This picture shows an Aztec sacrifice. The Aztecs sacrificed people in many different ways. In one rite, a young man impersonated the god Tezcatlipoca for a year; he was given everything he desired, including four beautiful girls as his wives, but at the end of that year he was sacrificed. On another occasion, captives were thrown into the fire alive but, before they died, were pulled out to have their hearts ripped from them. At the end of another ceremony, people took home the victims' flesh, and ate it in a stew.

Legacy of the Past

Some would argue that Hernan Cortes, the Spaniard who led the conquest of the Aztecs, destroyed one of the most remarkable civilizations in the world. The Aztecs were fearless warriors and great builders, who created an American empire that was only surpassed in size by that of the Incas in Peru. Their society was extremely well organized and stratified, and they had extensive trading networks. However, they were also invaders who stole the heritage and ideas of the peoples they replaced. Their technology was primitive, they terrorized the surrounding cities and sacrificed victims on a grand scale. Although the Spanish managed to wipe away much of their legacy, it is still possible to detect elements of the Aztec way of life in their modern day descendants, the Nahua, from the houses in which they live to the ways in which they worship.

HISTORICAL HOUSES

Many of the Aztec's descendants still live in houses very similar to the thatched, mud-brick cottages built by their ancestors. They still use traditional cooking, and traditional crafts. More than a million people speak Nahuatl, the language of the Aztecs and 19 out of every 20 modern-day Mexicans have some Aztec blood in their veins.

AZTEC PYRAMIDS

This is the Aztec 'Pyramid of the Sun' at Teotihuacan, a source of great inspiration to the Aztecs. On certain days of the year, the moving shadows of the setting sun made the pyramid appear to writhe. The Aztecs believed this reflected the movement of their snake-god, Quetzalcoatl.

THE DEMISE OF THE AZTECS

On Good Friday in 1519, Hernan
Cortes and 600 Spaniards landed on
the coast of Mexico. Just three years
later, the Aztec empire had surrendered
to them, and the city of Tenochtitlan
lay in ruins. Aztec weapons and battle
tactics were no match for the Spaniards,
who were helped by the Aztecs' many
enemies. And when the Aztecs, despite
all their sacrifices, were defeated by
the Spaniards, their morale collapsed;
their success and confidence depended
on their belief that the gods supported
them. One Aztec poem sadly ran:

Nothing but flowers and songs
of sorrow are left in Mexico

We are crushed to the ground;
we lie in ruins.

Have you grown tired of your servants?

Are you angry with your servants
O Giver of Life?

A NEW RELIGION

The Spaniards quickly destroyed the Aztec religion, and spread the message
of Christianity. Many Aztecs were happy to worship a God who did not
require constant sacrifice – but who had given Himself up to death instead,
so that humankind need not die. Today, many Nahua (descendents of the
Aztecs) are devoted Christians. But there are just a few Nahua who want
to return to the old religion, and traces of the old gods still survive in
some modern ceremonies. For instance, the Nahua still spread
marigolds on 2nd November, though they do so today
to celebrate the Christian festival of All Souls'
Day, not to honour Xochiquetzal.

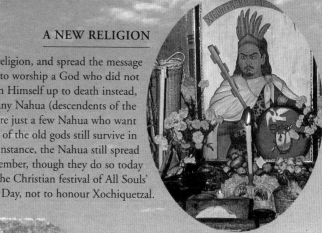

FIND OUT MORE

USEFUL WEBSITE ADDRESSES:

There is an excellent Aztecs web-site on:
http://northcoast.com/~spdtom/aztec.html

with a huge list of web links on:
http://northcoast.com/~spdtom/a-links.html

You can hear a Nahuatl greeting on:
http://www.public.iastate.edu/~rjsalvad/scmfaq/faqindex.html

Find out today's date in the Aztec calendar on:
http://www.azteccalendar.com/

PRONUNCIATION

This is how to say the names of the most popular Aztec gods:

Chalchiuhtlicue
(goddess of clean water and birth)
pronounced **Chal-chee-weet-lee-kway**
Chicomecoatl (corn goddess)
pronounced **Chee-co-me-co-atl**
Coatlicue (lady of the serpent skirt)
pronounced **Co-at-lee-kway**
Coyolxauhqui (moon goddess)
pronounced **Coy-ol-show-kee**
Huitzilopochtli (god of war)
pronounced **Weet-zil-o-potch-tly**

Macuilxochitl (god of plants and fun)
pronounced **Ma-kweel-sho-chitl**
Mictlantecuhtle (lord of the dead)
pronounced **Meek-tlan-tay-coot-ly**
Quetzalcoatl (Feathered Serpent, god of priests, creator)
pronounced **Kayt-zal-co-atl**
Tezcatlipoca (giver and taker of life)
pronounced **Tez-cat-li-po-ca**
Tlaloc (god of water and rain)
pronounced **Tlah-loc**
Tonatiuh (sun god)
pronounced **To-na-tee-oo**
Xilonen (goddess of the young corn)
pronounced **Shee-lo-nen**
Xipe Totec (god of spring and goldsmiths)
pronounced **Shee-pay To-tec**
Xochipilli (god of music, poetry, dance and flowers)
pronounced **Sho-chee-pee-ly**
Xochiquetzal (goddess of beauty, love and marigolds)
pronounced **Sho-chee-kay-tzall**
Yacatecuhtli (god of travellers)
pronounced **Ya-ca-tay-coot-ly**

ACKNOWLEDGEMENTS

We would like to thank: David Drew and Elizabeth Wiggans for their assistance. Artwork by John Alston and David Hobbs.
Copyright © 2000 ticktock Publishing Ltd.
First published in Great Britain by ticktock Publishing Ltd., The Offices in the Square, Hadlow, Tonbridge, Kent, TN11 0DD. All rights reserved.
No part of this publication may be reproduced, stored in a retrieval system, or transmitted in any form or by any means electronic, mechanical,
photocopying, recording or otherwise, without prior written permission of the copyright owner.
A CIP catalogue record for this book is available from the British Library. ISBN 1 86007 161 9 (paperback). ISBN 1 86007 228 3 (hardback).

Picture Credits:
t=top, b=bottom, c=centre, l=left, r=right, OFC=outside front cover, IFC=inside front cover, IBC=inside back cover, OBC=outside back cover

AKG; 2/3c, 2tl & OFC (main pic), 8c, 8/9cb, 11cl, 14tl, 16bl, 17t, 19c, 22bl & OBCtl,. Ancient Art & Architecture; OFCcb, 7br, 12tl, 18/19c, 29cl.
Ann Ronan @ Image Select; 13tr. Asia; 10cl. Corbis; 30/31 c. Elizabeth Baquedane; 9r, 14b, 18tl, 21br, 22/23c, 24t, 24tl, 28c, 31cr. et archive; OFCr, IFC,
2bl, 3bc, 3br, 5br, 5tr, 6/7c, 7tr, 8bl, 9t, 10br, 11br, 12tl, 13br & OBCcr, 15tl, 16tl, 17cl & OBCb, 19t, 24/25 & 32, 28/29c, p31ct. Image Select; 4c &
OFCc, 5br, 20/21 all. Planet Earth Pictures; 27c. Spectrum Colour Library; p8tl. Nick Saunders/Barbara Heller @ Werner Forman; 10cl. Werner Forman; 5c
& 29br, 6bm, 10tl, 12ct, 12/13tl, 23cr, 24r, 26tl, 26b, 26/27c, 28bl, 30cl.

Every effort has been made to trace the copyright holders and we apologize in advance for any unintentional omissions.
We would be pleased to insert the appropriate acknowledgement in any subsequent edition of this publication.

snapping-turtle
guide